Something Near the Dance Floor

Bruce Dethlefsen

Bruce Dethlefsen (signature)

Marsh River Editions

Copyright © 2003 by Bruce Dethlefsen

My grateful acknowledgment to the editors
of the following publications
in which some of these poems first appeared.

The Comstock Review: "The Rest of You"; *Free Verse:* "Dumped," "Every Needle," "Mineral Expectations," "Rage Walking," "White Stallions"; *Hands·On Drumming:* "Losing the Car Keys"; *Hepcat's Revenge:* "Fair Territory"; *Hodge Podge Poetry:* "Flickers"; *Hummingbird:* "Night Sands"; *North Coast Review:* "Monte Carlo"; *Seems:* "Dance Card"; *The TMP Irregular:* "The Penknife"
Books - *Between the Sheets* (Perma Press, 2002): "Fingernail Moon," "The House We Haunt Is Ours"; *Ring Them Bells* (Mid-State Poetry Towers, 2000)*:* "I'll Take the Moon"

ISBN 0-9718909-3-5
Publisher/Editor Linda Aschbrenner
Printed by Heinzen Printing Inc., Marshfield, Wisconsin

Marsh River Editions
M233 Marsh Road
Marshfield, WI 54449

for my sons,

Nathan and Wilson

Contents

Table for One	1
The Tree Story	2
Monte Carlo	4
Evening Wear	6
A Man of the World	8
Dumped	9
The Bone	10
The House We Haunt is Ours	12
The Rest of You	14
Losing the Car Keys	16
Rage Walking	17
The Car Salesman Hits His Stride at Fifty-five	18
Dance Card	19
Fair Territory	20
Flickers	22
Mineral Expectations	23
First Light	24
I'll Take the Moon	25
After a Year of Being Missing	26
The Penknife	27
Shebang	28
White Stallions	29
A Vacant Lot in Guatemala	30
Fingernail Moon	31
Mountain Dreams	32
Sulaco Night	33
Lover's Notes	34
Every Needle	35
To Bees or Not	36
Night Sand	37

Table for One

excuse me maitre d'
this is for you
      I need a smoke free table
      somewhere closer to the music
      with an unobstructed view
so please amuse me
choose me
something near the dance floor

The Tree Story

the wind was from the west the sunset wind
it came to knock the backyard pine tree down

the tree swayed back and forth a couple times
it rocked it buckled then it snapped in three
the pine tree fell forever then the thud

the neighbors cocked their heads this way and that
at the enormous wrongness of the thing
that lay across the lawn one neighbor said
how tired it must have been and luckily
the poor tree didn't land on someone's head

I took an ax and chopped the tree by hand
the neighbor brought his chain saw by to help
you never have to do this by yourself

we stacked the bigger logs for firewood
it takes about a year for them to dry

the stump remained I dug at it for days
exposing every root I sliced each one
and tried to pull it from the hole with chains
but every time I pulled the chains gave way
the stump's too big a job to do myself
I'll have to ask somebody else for help

my marriage grew and fell for sixteen years
I can't remember who it was yelled timber
nor precisely when but there were tears
enough to put out fires every ember

one night next june my son and I will sit
beside each other at the burning pit
he'll ask to hear the story of the tree
and how the west wind came again last summer
I'll tell him one more time he never tires
and choose another log to feed the fire

Monte Carlo

at fourteen and a half
he thinks the future's wholly
one full tank of gas

just nuts about some monte carlo
parked inside the third row
of a used car lot in green bay

the car's a two-toned job
he's told one owner
a retired polish catholic mechanic
from the chevrolet garage
who drove it only
to the packer games on sunny days
at least until the funeral
of his wife and not again

imagine dad
an eighty-three
with sixty thousand actual miles
for under a thousand dollars
but they say they'll take
nine hundred cash

the boy the car
conceived and manufactured
at the same moment exactly

the cream and green boy
revved up gassed up
hitting on all eight cylinders
his eyes on high beam
braces chrome and sparkle

I smile
kick his tires for luck
pat his hood and climb on board
the father
the car
into the sun we slowly coast

Evening Wear

it wasn't stealing really
I just borrowed my son's wristwatch
to wear to the board meeting

he forgot it though I thought it
was on purpose when we went back
to his mother's house on sunday
we're often late and leave in haste

I saw it right away when I got home
it had a steel blue face and golden trim
a silver twist-o-flexible band
with a golden strand that ran around it

the fit was perfect
our wrists are the same size now
although I wish the watch smelled more like him

at the meeting I daydreamed of my son
and felt the tap dance
on the ghost strings stretched between us

that night I wore my son as evening wear
the way some women
wear their man's clothes
when they're gone

my son is my accessory
I need to have him with me
and against me
bound skin to skin
manacled if need be

A Man of the World

a skilled sewer will hand-stitch
fifty-eight baseballs
in a single ten hour shift

my son will celebrate
the bicentennial of the civil war
and far beyond
if he can afford the parts

a chinese dissident's kidney or liver
columbian lungs
some poor ethiopian's heart

for truth he'll be a man of the world

with skin from tanganyikans
(or do they go by other names now?)
a pancreas from panama
a leg from lagos
a liberian rib
an armenian arm

the cold quiet eye of eskimo

the closest I could ever come to immortality
was a five dollar japanese catcher's mitt
and horsehide costa rican baseball
but then
I was barely alive
when babe ruth died

Dumped

you've fallen from my train of thought
you flew off in the night
tumbled over and over
skidded and crumpled to rest
among the gravel and ties
between the tracks

did it hurt a lot?

I'm a little curious
cause I've been dumped
a time or two myself

did you have a chance
to look back even for a second?
did you see the light?
feel the rumble in the rails?
hear the quickening whistle?

you must have seen it coming

I have to admit
I did push a bit

The Bone

men are dogs
they sing the same songs dogs do
and understand about as many words
they look this way and that way
as they eat from their bowls

they say some are trainable

they sniff at every tree to check their messages
and circle when they make their beds

about the bone
don't touch the bone
don't ask about the bone
don't try to find it
and never use the bone as a toy

men require licenses
they chase after cars and bury things
they run together to nip in play
and bite when they mean business
one bark will set off a whole neighborhood
of men all night

you can call them
they have names
like bob and lucky and lumumba
and sometimes they will come

yes there are good dogs and there are bad dogs

they constantly scratch themselves
and of course they'd lick themselves if they could
they wear collars
and dig holes on hot days to lie in

you can pet them and rub them behind the ears
all you want
but remember
men are dogs
don't go near the bone
don't joke about the bone
leave the bone alone

The House We Haunt is Ours

we wander through the corridors
inside the middle of the night
in little hours

I toss
she turns
we flail our arms and knees in bed
we kick at covers
spiders do the backstroke in a pool

all I need is time to write
some time to think
to get the manuscript together
I have to write better
that's the answer
writing better

she never thought she'd have no family
live unmarried
have no money
be unhappy
nuns have better sex lives

she comes back to bed and I get up
and I come back then she gets up
we alternate like this all night
shift workers at the abandoned slumber mill
    the haunted house
sleepily we punch in
we punch out

separate we descend the creaky stairs
float floor to floor
swim room to room
we roam and write
check e-mail watch tv
burnt popcorn treads butter in a bowl
we stroll the blacktop
looking for our car
the keys
in the yellow lighted empty parking lot
outside the silent factory

the grinding little hours
the crawling hours
the cobweb hours
blinking in the darkness

so few words pass between us
at the gate in the chain link fence
no gestures
waves
no overtures
I whistle and I swing my lunch pail back to work
as she heads home alone to warm the bed
we haunt the little hours
that pass for night

The Rest of You

most of you shook out
onto your parents' graves in allouez
the rest except a tablespoon or so
I used to dust the adolescent
pepper and tomato plants
just as the sun set on the garden

that was what you told me
that was what you wished
and now I had some left

all night I worried whether I should use you
as a foot powder
so I could walk with you inside my shoes
wherever I might go
or daub you on my groin to avoid chafing
it seemed almost appropriate

maybe mix you up with baker's clay
and form an amulet
to wear you on a chain around my neck

and while I was consumed with what to do with you
the rest of you
I spooned you with some sugar on my shredded wheat
I added milk
and ate you in a bowl of cereal

you tasted good

and that's how I'll remember you
with sprinkles

Losing the Car Keys

new drummer
that I am
I warm up and join in
skin on skin
slip into the mayhem
the rhythm and listen
I have to hear what I drum
so I can tell
which one is me

and when I find myself drumming
that's when I hear the others
and lose myself drumming
that's when we're there

that's when my hands disappear
and the drum disappears
and my car keys
tuh tuh dum,
and your lover
tuh tuh dum
and even we disappear
disappear
tuh tuh dum

Rage Walking

I didn't have anything else to do
so I decided to take a walk around the lake
on the path where I always go
just past the beach up ahead I see this guy
and he's pushing a kid in a stroller
he was a nice enough looking guy
walking pretty slow
I couldn't tell for sure but I think they were from illinois
and as I start to pass them
the kid throws this stuffed animal thing
out of the stroller onto the path
this white furry thing right where I was going to pass
I almost have to stop then cause the guy's reaching for it
but he can't reach it cause he's trying to move the stroller
over to the right with his other hand
finally he swoops down and snags it
stands back up and looks at me kind of stupid
well by now I'm stopped
and he just stands there gawking at me
and he doesn't move
and I mean he wouldn't move
so I shot him

The Car Salesman
Hits His Stride at Fifty-five

gone are the gold tooth
the chains the medallion
the white patent leather

the day is new
I'm a salesperson
and I have something to sell
I'm a salesperson
and I will sell
sell it all

first myself
then the dream the feel
then the sheet metal

here comes the customer
remember
touch his shoulder
smile but no eye contact
be cheerful to the gourdhead
then tell him what he wants

beam for the chrissake

Dance Card

the musical selections
were interrupted by the news
about our victorian neighbor
who had upped and hanged herself

of course we said
how sad too bad
it's tragic and how could she
and I thought how I'd been taught

to finish off the throw
the game the season
complete each lesson every class
hang in there
to be in it to the last
and sit enduring every play
until the curtain falls
until the death of the applause

but maybe someone else's program's shorter
not so many notes and chords before the coda
who has a small but ample dance card
listing partners filled to overflowing

one full brocaded dance card
dangling by the braided thread
as the music resumes in a cool waltz
around a blue wrist

Fair Territory

it wasn't the peanut butter and jelly blood
that dripped from his chin so much
as it was the nervous urine that spread
from one of his red ball jets
across the white painted foul line
of the playground blacktop

when george the greek kid got goofy
and went nutso over something in our kickball game
his eyes snapped open so quick
it stretched the nostrils of his pasty face
he'd stand with one foot in fair territory
half hunched over
and clench the index knuckle of his fist
between his teeth and tug
like wild dogs will tear apart
the youngest weakest antelope
its thin limp carcass
bouncing up and down
and back and forth
the way enraged ventriloquists might fight over a dummy

when we saw that elbow flapping
we knew that george was doing his darnedest
to stifle the scream
that always followed
and that perhaps it was a good idea
to steer clear a bit
at least for another couple outs

jesus george
if only paul winchell
could hold you in his lap
just for a second
and slide one cool hand
up your back

Flickers

for Harold Brodkey

go back to sleep
it's not tomorrow yet

no
what you're hearing on the bridge
is not the sound
of pigeons passing overhead
nor whispered whistle
of women pissing
you just think you hear the beat of wings

no
what you see
is not the flutterings of daylight
it's projection
you're an actor in a movie
you remember
the one with the cast
of a thousand shadows

now
go back to sleep
go back and dream some
dream perhaps of mourning doves
of mourning doves
and flickers

Mineral Expectations

limestone awfully lonesome
since my father's gone
and miss our little talcs
and conversations

how I marbled
at the strength of this good man
a grocer who would sandstone much all day
that he developed varicosities
in both his legs and never once complained

even though I took his love for granite
I can still recoal his exact words and sediments

it slate for him he'd say too late
but you shale mica difference in this world
he'd point at me and shake his finger

of quartz he understood and wished for me
not just the same old schist
but a future that pyrites
would be mined
and mined alone

First Light

I have failed to fill
the feeder for a week
I'm sorry

the frosted leaves fall so fast
past the barren
crab apple branches

I thought you were birds at first
I hoped you were
yellow birds and red birds

how dare you survive
without me

I'll Take the Moon

for Henry Hart

if someone will take the sun
and you say will do water
and maybe somebody else try the earth
or love or wind
or sex or war
or fire birds or flowers
then I'll take the moon
and dedicate what's left of my life
to capture keep show and tell
utterly and complete
the epic story of the moon
but first
I need somebody to take the other things
otherwise it'll be too much for me

come on then
you take the sun
come on now
take the sun

After a Year of Being Missing

they tested the bones in las vegas
for dna and it was her brother all right
she said he'd always had the biggest dreams
I'm so sorry we asked
was he older than you?
well he used to be
but after a year of being missing
no one could tell

the bones had some effects with them
they were sure it was him
when they tested my niece and nephew for dna

now we're worried about her too she said
frank's daughter was involved in a colt
you know
a bunch of people with crazy ideas
oh a cult we said together a cult

I knew he had gone off to die she said
when we saw him last at gertie's funeral
I know people can just go off and die
the surprise was
that he was murdered
not really a surprise though
because I knew
he was going off to die anyway

she sealed the wadded kleenex
back in the ziplock bag on the table
and now I need some sympathy she said

The Penknife

the day I was ten
I found a flashlight
and a penknife
wrapped inside
this note from my father
who I hadn't seen in nine years
under a rock
by the sidewalk

these are the five rules of life it said
        overlight – comedy
        underlight – horror
        backlight – romance
        no light – film noir
        cut
love dad

Shebang

these people
these place
these time of day

these breeze oh ain't they sweet
these air to breathe
these sun wet world
these whole big blue green deal

and then these night
these children moon
these stars on strings
these stars
these twang of things

teewang

White Stallions

the children of the street
must see themselves
in the greasy puddles of the forenoon
in the sundown storefront windows
in the luster of the shoes they shine

must see themselves
in the reflection of a customer's sunglasses
in the tears of the old women
in the shadow of the bus

the children of the street
must see themselves
flying purple kites on sunny beaches
dining with the family after church
riding white stallions

the children of the street
must see themselves

(Quetzaltenango, Guatemala 1998)

A Vacant Lot in Guatemala

a harmony of rats and roses
fills the vacant lot next door
with music separated from the world
by walls of brown adobe

the music rises
as the roses shuffle
in the wind of the volcano
their thorns outstretched
to claw and scratch the walls

the music rises
as the rats sway
crooning in the ocean breeze
a honeyed melody
against a sky of blue and white

and each red petal falls
onto the yellow teeth of the marimba
producing notes though sweet
become the elemental horror of the song

because all roses smell of rats
and rats of roses

(Quetzaltenango, Guatemala 1998)

Fingernail Moon

todos los poetas son lunáticos

we agreed that we'd look up
and find the moon to say goodnight
you at ten o'clock
me at nine
me in guatemala
you in wisconsin

I'd been tv switching back and forth
between lassie barking español
and couples calling in describing
just then
how they were making love

at nine o'clock I opened the window
and looked out past volcán santa maría
to see only low slung scratchy clouds
that smelled of yellow diesel fumes
the color of corn and the flavor of corn

so how'd it go for you?

I hope you saw the moon hang in the sky
somehow tonight
if only but a fingernail
I know now why all poets are lunatics

good night

(Guatemala City 1998)

Mountain Dreams

you have mountain dreams
the mountain tells you bring your people

the green tongues of the leaves
say bring those you know

the blue teeth of the clouds
say bring those you never knew

the purple lips of fruit
say bring those you love

the brown mouths of the wood
say bring those who are dead

the mountain shrugs his shoulders
it's not important he says
bring who you want
we'll pile them up
dream your little dreams
it's all the same to me

(Tegucigalpa, Honduras 2002)

Sulaco Night

the end of the day
I rest
leveled by the press of sun
the rain or dust
I place
my head on the pillow
of the exhausted poet
who wrote before me
his breath
still thick in the air
his words
crawling on adobe walls
each empty space
between the words
a drop of sweat suspended
hanging in the darkness

(Sulaco, Yoro, Honduras 2002)

Lover's Notes

here's the love note I wrote her

> each breath we take is but a token
> what we've written wrote in reddest blood
> when the awoken heart is broken
> and every word unspoken spoken
> so I guess I love you

okay I didn't say it was any good

I folded the note with mild dread
and slid it slowly down the bench
she opened it and read it

then she stood and said
what's this some kind of arfing joke?
and slapped me remotely
upside the head

see I told you I told myself
and wrote me a note suggesting

> next time you're so amorously smitten
> either get yourself a better love
> or write your love notes better written

Every Needle
for Mary Beth

you say since you were little
in the christmas dark
you lay on your back
much like a present
looking up beyond each branch
each light and ornament
until you see the silver star
so far away atop the tree

gee
you are the only other
person in this world who does
and I have found you

I remember every needle

will you marry me?

I want to lie with
you beneath the tree

To Bees or Not

a poet plays with words
the way a sculptor plays with clay
the way a picture taker
makes his thumbs a frame

the way an undertaker
plays with smiles
a poker player plays with piles
the way expectant parents
try on different names

how the drummer slaps his knees
why the beekeeper hums or not
to bees
there is no question
the artist's hardest work
is mostly play

Night Sand

I draw each moon word
in the night sand of the beach
reluctantly

I hope I never
though the tides erase all trace
lose this lunacy

Bruce Dethlefsen was born in Kansas City, Missouri, in 1948. He moved to Wisconsin in 1966 and attended college in La Crosse and Oshkosh. His first chapbook, *A Decent Reed*, was published by Tamafyhr Mountain Press.

Bruce lives in Westfield and is currently the director of the public library in Montello where he organizes monthly readings.

He says the flying dreams are his favorite.

SOMETHING NEAR THE DANCE FLOOR

by Bruce Dethlefsen
was printed in an edition of 300 copies.
It is the fourth publication of Marsh River Editions.
Series design by Nicholas Aschbrenner.